Killer Creative Instincts

How To Harness Your Creative Skills Into A Marketable, Money Making Business

By Landon T. Smith

Copyright 2017 by Landon T. Smith

Published by Make Profits Easy LLC

Profitsdaily123@aol.com

facebook.com/MakeProfitsEasy

Table of Contents

Introduction 4

Chapter 1: Killing the Starving Artist 7

Chapter 2: Artistic Startups 20

Chapter 3: Running Your Dream Like a Business
.... 33

Chapter 4: The Wonder Twins of the Digital
Revolution 58

Chapter 5: Marketing Makes Perfect 74

Conclusion 96

Introduction

What's the difference between an artist and a large pizza? A large pizza can feed a family of four! We might all laugh at these kinds of jokes, jokes that equate working in the creative field to working for free, but there is a profound truth to the phrase starving artist. If you didn't know any better, you might actually believe that you can't make a living off of your art. Yet, the traditional picture of the hippy artist who's slaving away for years without seeing a paycheck is on the way out, and that is because of one simple reason: the digital revolution is changing everything.

You see, a long time ago, there was really only one way for the artist to be able to make a buck and that was to find someone who had access to distribution. This fat cat often had the networks and money to spread an artist's works around, but at a tremendous cost. Who hasn't heard the story of an artist or creative type losing his valuable rights just because the record label or publisher had all the power? Things back then were really painful and made making a living as an artist all about the concept of discovery.

But all that is changing and it's changing for the better! The purpose of this book is to teach you to ditch the word "artist" and instead adopt the word "artist operator" that is, someone who's not just willing to create his art, but also willing to treat his art as a business! You will find the secrets to how you can take advantage of the digital revolution, bypass the gatekeepers who have traditionally stopped anyone from becoming successful without them and learn what it means to become an independent business owner. If you are an artist who's always been looking for a way to make money, then stop looking because this book has everything you need to know about how to make it in the new economy. Let's head on over to the first chapter where we will kill a few myths and rumors that have been keeping the artist down for over a century!

Chapter 1: Killing the Starving Artist

So you want to make a living off of your art? Great! So let's work out some definitions first, before we get into the meat of the book. When I say art, I mean any creative endeavor that you are pursuing. So whether you are crafting custom made jewelry out of sea shells, making paintings, writing books or even making music, art applies to any of these concepts.

Now, there are two types of artists who make art, starving artists and artist operators. You definitely want to be an artist operator and you certainly want to avoid becoming a starving artist. What's the difference between the two? Truthfully, the difference is simply a state of mind. In order to understand what to become, you must be willing to learn what makes a starving artist so unsuccessful.

The starving artist looks at his work as part of a sacred process and believes that art itself will get him success. He focuses all of his time and energy on his art and very little time on the business part. He believes that discovery plays a huge part in success and so he slaves away on his art, working on piece after piece in the hopes of some day making it big. And in the meantime, he suffers. He suffers immensely, either financially by being broke, or emotionally by being forced to work a job that he hates just to make ends meet. But each day, his dreams of one day making it will propel him forward. But ten years go by and he still isn't where he wants to be.

Now, that seems like quite a bleak picture, doesn't it? Well, you might be in that category. Most artists, especially the younger ones, traditionally are. They focus on getting their art perfected and creating the best possible art so that they may one day be discovered. They dream endless dreams of getting that email, or phone call that tells them "hey, I think you're amazing, let's get you into the big leagues!" They surround themselves by stories of people who get discovered and spend a great deal of time waiting for their number to finally come up.

But what exactly is the concept of discovery? What makes it so attractive to the artist, so much so that they are willing to put all of their hope on being discovered? Let's break down what it means to be discovered, and in the process, we will learn how the system is actually rigged against the majority of us.

The traditional idea of discovery comes from the process of sending in products to the gatekeepers. These gatekeepers are the people who have access to all of the information networks that you would need to be heard and seen by other people. A gatekeeper could be a book publisher, a literary agent, an art curator or a record label. They have the ability to make people successful by distributing their art around the country or in some cases, the world. They often have the finances and the resources to back up such a risky investment. When someone says they want to be discovered, what they really mean is that they want a gatekeeper to take interest in them and help them reach distribution. An aspiring actress might want an agent to get her good roles in films, an author might want to have his book picked up by one of the Big Five in publishing.

Discovery depends on several different factors and only one of them you can actually control. For a gatekeeper to discover you, they must like your product, have a willingness to invest in you, believe that your product will make money and that you can produce more products for them. In other words, you must prove your economic viability to them before they are even willing to give you a chance. To make matters worse, *it doesn't even matter if your product is actually good.* Yikes. Is that true? Well, stop for a moment and think of the great many pieces of art out there that aren't very good yet have become commercial hits. Think about things such as the Twilight Series or those 50 Shades of Grey books. Surely, your work must be better than that, right? One should hope so!

But we find that marketability, sell ability, return on investment, etc. are all pieces of what a gatekeeper is looking for. To be discovered isn't to mean that you are excellent, but rather that you can sell. And best of all, the gatekeeper also takes the lion's share of the profits. The standard rate for authors from most publishing deals is maybe 10 percent total. That means 90% of the blood, sweat and tears that you poured into your work is now being taken by the gatekeepers who have the power to, at any moment, cut you loose and leave you high and dry.

So the concept of discovery tells us all that we too can be found and not only can we be found, but all of our dreams can also come true, but at such a hefty price. In the old days, that was the only system available, because distribution was impossible to achieve at an individual level. If you were an artist, you didn't have much of a chance to also be a distributor due to the sheer cost involved.

Discovery makes sense, for an economy where physical distribution was the only method of distribution available. However, now that the internet has arrived in full swing, things are an entirely different story. Now, we are finding out that the gatekeepers who once held the keys to the kingdom of greatness, can easily be circumvented, but at a cost. You see, if we were to sum up the concept of discovery into a single word, that word would be luck. There is a great deal of luck involved in being discovered and no matter how skilled you are, how beautiful your work is or how excellent you are at your craft, it all boils down to someone seeing your work at the right time, in the right mood and in the right circumstances.

How then, are we to make a living off of luck? How then are we to make a living out of waiting for the dice to roll in our favor? Well, there is an alternative to waiting for random chance to save us from destitution and in my opinion, it is far better than the process of discovery. The solution is for us to take the reins ourselves and learn how to be an artist operator.

You see, the starving artist relies on forces outside of his control in order to become successful. This isn't to say that he's bad or lazy, that's just how the old system has worked. But now there is a new system in place, one for the artist operator to thrive in.

So what is an artist operator? Simply put, he is someone who looks at his artistic endeavor as a business and treats it as such. Instead of putting all of his energy and dedication into his craft, which is very important, he puts his energy into the business side of what he does. This ensures that he will be able to make a living off of his work, instead of having to wait to be discovered. There is a beauty in this transition from starving artist to artist operator, because it gives you the ultimate power over your own destiny. The artist operator doesn't look to be discovered, instead he looks to sell.

Yikes! I said the S word! Before we move any further, there is something that must be addressed and it is quite prevalent in the artist community, especially among those who treasure their work and reject the modern principles of commercialism. There can be a tension, within the heart of an artist, to sell and to create. Often times, the business aspect of being an artist is overlooked or ignored entirely because it is a very uncomfortable thing to focus on. We don't want to be sellouts or to lose our artist integrity, and so we avoid anything that looks remotely close to compromising our artist beliefs. Yet, we are also shooting ourselves in the foot when we shun the concept of looking at art as a business, because we are *denying people who would love our work the opportunity to consume it.*

Most artists look for discovery because it removes all of the pressure of having to sell and advertise, instead leaving the artist alone to focus purely on making their art. This is a noble endeavor, but the problem is that this leaves you forever waiting for discovery. If you are perfectly fine with rolling the dice time and time again, that's fine. You won't get any more help out of this book because this book is not for the artist who is only willing to work on his art. This book is for the artist operator who has come to realize that if he wants to be successful, he will have to develop a business mindset as well.

Of course, you don't have to like the business aspect at all. But if you want to be successful, you will have to be willing to roll your sleeves up and get to work. Ideally, you will be able to reach a point of success where you can hire other people to do the business stuff for you, but in the very beginning, it's just you and your work ethic.

So you have a choice. You can say goodbye to being a starving artist, put to bed any dreams of discovery and get to work, or you can stay where you are and hope that the odds come up in your favor. This is where the rubber meets the road. Both choices are fine, honestly, but it's more about what you want. Do you want to have guaranteed success in your artistic endeavor? Then you must choose the harder path. Only those who fight inch by inch for new territory will be able to later reap the rewards. The only way you can be sure that you can be a successful artist is to take the reins and start doing it yourself.

Or you can hang back and continue to focus on your art. Art is good, but the fact is, there is a literal ocean of it in this world. You might be amazing at what you do, but how will you be found without discovery? Choose now, who you want to be. An artist operator will move on to the next chapter and begin to look at themselves in an entirely new light.

Chapter 2: Artistic Startups

If you made it to this chapter, congratulations! You are now one step closer to becoming an artist operator and that means you are one step closer to becoming a real success! But it takes more than a willingness to get your hands dirty in order to become a successful artist operator, it also takes a willingness to change your perspective.

So let's approach this new endeavor from the ground up, reimagining everything that you know about your art. There are three noble truths to know about being an artist operator and if you can follow these three noble truths, you will have the makings of success. Failure to follow these truths will mean that you aren't going to live up to your potential as an artist operator. Of course, there are plenty more steps involved in becoming a success, but in order to reach those other steps, you must first have the groundwork laid out.

Noble Truth One: You are a Business

You are a business. There is no getting around this. If we are to become artist operators, then we must realize that your own state of being is nothing more than being part of a start up company. Now, that company is designed to sell a product, that is, your art, but it is important that we realize this as soon as possible. You are not just an author, a painter, an illustrator or a musician, you are the sole proprietor of your very own business. That means you must also be willing to look at everything you do as part of your businesses operations. This means that you must have a strategy, a business plan, a vision and measurables to make sure that you are functioning well. You must have your finances in order and look at your professional life as if it were a day job.

Ugh, day jobs suck, right? Wrong! A day job is perfectly fine, when it's the thing that you want to do. There can be a temptation, when you are an artist, to believe that other jobs suck, but the truth is there are a great many people out in the world who enjoy what they are doing, despite the fact that to an artist it might be soul crushing. There is nothing wrong with looking at your artistic endeavor as a job, because ideally, it is the thing that you want to be doing full time. So treat it as such and you will go far.

Noble Truth Two: You make a product

Now, this one might sting a bit, but when it comes to being an artist, we can often look at our work as something that is sacred. It's tough, because there is often a large emotional toll when it comes to creating our work. We sacrifice a lot of time, energy and effort into the work, infusing everything that we have into it and by the end of the creation process, we look at our artistic piece as being a part of us. No one wants to have that piece then labeled as a product to be thrown up on a shelf.

But let's think in realistic business terms here. Regardless of what your art is, if you are planning on selling it in exchange for financial gain, then your art is a product. The word product, of course, can make us feel a little uncomfortable. It can make us feel as if our work is nothing more than a box of Q-Tips to be sold at a local Walmart and that is understandable. No one wants their work of art to be equated to a piece of merchandise. However, let us learn how to change our perspective on what the word product truly means.

A product is consumed by the consumer. No matter what that product is, its entire purpose is meant to be consumed, interacted with and enjoyed by a consumer. The entire purpose of a product is to be enjoyed by someone else, and doesn't that stay the same for us as artists? How many of us wish to create our work and then stuff it away for no one else to see? If that were the case, and you wished to hide your work from the rest of the world, why then are you reading a book on making money off of your craft?

The truth is, you have a choice. You can focus entirely on yourself or you can focus on the person who will get to enjoy your work. Most people in the world don't mind paying for something they enjoy, so what is the hold up? Oftentimes, we don't look at our art as products because we feel that it demeans our work, but I would propose to you that if you were to look at your art as a product, it would allow for better consumer access.

That's the real truth about treating your art as a product: people won't get access to it any other way. You want others to be able to enjoy what you make, and thanks to the power of the internet, you have the opportunity to reach as many people as possible. No matter what you make, there is a market for you somewhere. But you must be willing to shift away from the art mindset to the business mindset. Art happens when you put your energy into making the product, but afterwards must come the business mindset. That is the only way you will be able to survive which brings us to the last point.

Noble Truth Three: Money Is Number One

And here is where we go against the traditional advice that "money can't buy you happiness." Truthfully, money is the life blood of any business. Try to convince a Fortune 500 company that money isn't important and watch what happens. You'd be laughed out of the board room. Money is an absolute necessity if you want to survive and interact with the world around you. You have no influence in the world if you have no money. That's an unfortunate truth about the world that we live in. Money makes the world go round and there is no going against that.

If you believe that you are a business, then it goes to show that you must also accept the fact that making money should be your number one priority in that business. The reason for this, of course, is the fact that if you can't make money, you won't be able to make more art. Let's be honest, if you are fueled by your art, you most likely won't derive satisfaction from working at a 9-5 that takes you away from what you want to do. No artist wants to work a day job that makes them spend the majority of their time and energy living someone else's dream.

But if you aren't putting importance on making a paycheck from your work, you will never get to where you want to be. The fact remains, money is our only way to interact with the world. It is a necessity and nothing you can do in this world will change the fact that you need it to be able to function.

Let us not deny the value and power of money. When we have a lot of it, we are able to do a great amount of good in the world and most importantly, we are able to focus on our art, unfettered. Money would allow for you to expand your business, hire other people to manage the business aspect of your company and pay for advertising.

Yet, there has been such a hesitation in the artist community to look at money for the value it can provide, primarily because we often see the negative effects of a cash grab in the modern art world. Everyone can tell when a filmmaker phones it in to make a couple of bucks off of low effort work, or when an artist doesn't really give everything because they are interested in making low quality work to cash in on some kind of trend. While it is true that we should not allow our motivation for money to affect our artistic integrity, that doesn't mean that we are required to not think about the money at all. At the end of the day, if you are going to be an artist operator, then you must be someone who is able to make money for yourself. There is no getting around it.

The trick is to learn how to divide your focus evenly. When you are creating your artistic endeavor, you should focus on that entirely. Don't give thought to making cash just yet, instead focus on creating it for your purposes and focus all of your time and energy on doing the job well. Then, after you have made your product, whatever it is, you can then begin to think about how you are going to sell it. But if you say "I'm not in this business to make money," then you are going to fulfill that prophecy no matter what. Money matters and there is no avoiding this fact.

So do these three truths change your perspective of what your actual role is as an artist operator? Creating art is really only one part of the equation, there is an entirely different world that exists separate from the art-making process that is the most vital part of being an artist operator. In the next chapter, we'll look at how to start focusing on your work as a business, so that you can start making money.

Chapter 3: Running Your Dream Like a Business

Once you have come to the conclusion that your artistic pursuit is meant to be treated like a business, it changes how you approach your work. Instead of focusing purely on your art, you will discover that there is now a brand new section that you will need to put your time, effort and energy into: the business itself. This whole section is about introducing you to the concept of how to run your dream like a business and how to treat it differently from how a starving artist would.

The starving artist's approach to their work is more akin to a hobbyist approach, when you think about it. They have no business plan, no goals other than discovery and worst of all, they tend to have tremendously good work ethic that doesn't go anywhere. If you want to be a successful artist operator then you must be willing to put as much work and effort as you possibly can into the business aspect of what you are doing. It is the only way to reach long lasting success.

So with that in mind, let's go ahead and start breaking down the concept of business principles that you will need to follow if you want to make it to success. Once you have these principles figured out and put together in a clear and concise manner, you will be able to have a real shot at achieving greatness in your lifetime. Let's get started.

Business Principle One: Have a vision

Business philosophy 101 dictates that the growth capacity of any kind of company, be it an ice-cream company or a Fortune 500 company is affected heavily by their vision. A vision is essentially a picture of what you want to be in the future. The vision drives any good company forward to be as successful as possible. Everything is done in pursuit of the vision.

Likewise, if you are going to be operating as a business, regardless of what your art is, then you must have a vision for the future. What does the future look like to you? Do you have your own shop where you can sell your wares? Are you a well known literary author? Are you working in the film business full time? No matter what the vision is, you must have one and it must be strong enough and compelling enough to motivate you to move forward.

There are going to be rough times for you in the future, there is no doubt about that. The path of the self-made individual isn't an easy one, and as such, you are going to need to have a strong vision of what the future looks like for you. The stronger the vision, the easier it is to endure hardship, disappointment, frustration and other sorrows that can discourage and prevent us from accomplishing our dreams.

So think long and hard about what your vision for the future is. Don't simply think about vision as some kind of daydream about the future, however, because it is something that you are actively working towards to accomplish. The vision must be realistic, possible and achievable within the future for you. It will require some practical thinking, of course, and it must have an honest timeline, but you will see that a meticulously constructed vision will open the door to accomplishing things that you never knew possible.

When building a vision, it is important to be able to answer questions about what the future will look like for you. Try to include as many specifics as possible, including income, work status, hours you'll need to work each week, etc. The better picture that you have of what your goals are, the more inclined you will be to adapt strategies to reach those goals which brings us to the next section.

Business Principle Two: Have A Strategy

Once you have your vision worked out, you should be able to draw out several goals from there. For example, if you want to be able to employ another person to work for you, you might have the goal of make 30k so I can hire someone to work full time for me. It's important to have a broken down and tangible list of goals that will allow you to focus on building a strategy to reach those goals.

Remember: a goal is not a strategy. No matter how many goals you have, unless you are able to put together a comprehensive strategy to achieve them, they aren't worth much. In other words, not only must you have a dream, you must also learn how to plot a course to make those dreams come true. This is an entirely different affair from building goals, because goals are really focused on what you want. Strategies are focused entirely on the *how*.

And here is where things become a little more complicated for yourself as an artist operator. No doubt you already know how to work on your craft and that you can do it quite well, you probably don't need anyone to tell you how to create art. However, you might not be terribly knowledgeable on how to achieve your business related strategies. For example, if you want to sell 1,000 copies of your book, you are going to need to learn how to build a strategy to do that. Many starving artists look at this charge, to roll up your sleeves and do the hard work, to be intimidating and overwhelming. Since they don't have the natural instincts to figure it out, they instead shut down and say "I don't know how."

But the truth is, we exist in a world where we have access to immense amounts of information at the touch of a button. Your laptop or smart phone is able to tell you everything that you need in order to be able to figure out how to build specific types of strategies. Now, we won't dig into specific strategies for specific types of artistic endeavors because there are far too many to even consider, but we will talk about the most valuable tool that you have in your toolbox as an artist operator. That tool is the ability to learn.

It is unfortunate, but the traditional education system has sold us a lie. We were told growing up that the most important thing to know is information, we were drilled relentlessly to memorize facts and figures and were graded on the information that we were able to regurgitate flawlessly. We were not taught that the most important part of learning is knowing how to learn. And so there are a great many of us who, when confronted with the unknown, tend to freeze up and perform poorly. Don't fall into the trap of thinking that information memorized is the most important part of being intelligent. Memorization plays only a tiny role in intelligence. The smartest people, the sharpest CEOs and those who are truly successful make their way not by memorizing, but by learning how to learn.

So how do we learn how to learn? As paradoxical as it might seem, it really just takes an open mind and a willingness to approach the challenge of learning new things as a puzzle to unlock instead of an obstacle to overcome. Oftentimes we tend to look at our lack of knowledge about something as some kind of barrier, but what would happen if we were to treat it as a puzzle instead? What if you were trying to figure out how to acquire a company, and you treated that as if it were some kind of game to figure out? What would you do differently? How many of us try to solve puzzles and get frustrated because we don't know the answer? The entire purpose of a puzzle is to get us to figure it out and likewise, the entire purpose of learning how to learn is to figure things out for ourselves. You have the resources and the technology to learn anything that you like, but its up to you. So as you begin to develop strategies, each time that you hit a wall, don't fret or despair, instead buckle down and become determined to solve the problem. You will be far better for it.

Business Principle Three: Time is your most important resource

Time is a fickle thing, it can slip away at a moment's notice if you don't pay attention. Not only is time fickle, but it is also one of the most important resources in our lives. Time moves at a perpetual rate, and each second that slips away will never be regained. You cannot buy more time, no matter how much money you have. You cannot get your hours wasted back. And since we cannot do anything to gain more time in our days, we must realize that it is the single most valuable resource that we have in our artist operator arsenal. Because money is finite, it comes and goes, some days you'll be broke and some days you'll be wealthy, but ultimately it changes based on what you do. Time doesn't work the same way, we all get the same set amount of time each day.

In a way, you are extremely wealthy with your time. You can choose to spend it however you like. So if you want to watch a movie, you can spend 2 hours out of your allotted 24 to enjoy a film. But when you do so, that time will never come back, so you must be cautious and careful as to not waste your time. Now, the value of your time is in direct proportion to what else you could be doing. For example, if someone offered you 20 bucks to mow the lawn for an hour but you chose instead to browse the internet for an hour, the value of your time was 20 bucks and you actually chose the less economically valuable thing by wasting time on YouTube. This is what we refer to as opportunity cost.

Now, assuming that your start as an artist operator isn't a completely lucrative endeavor quite yet, you might not see your time working on your business as very valuable. After all, if it's not making money, what good is it? Well, in terms of immediate payoff, you are correct, spending 2 hours watching television instead of spending 2 hours of working on your business has the exact same immediate value, but what about long term value? What is the investment value of both activities?

Spending 2 hours on your business means that you are investing 2 hours of hard work into your future. Those hours will compound over time. 2 hours wasted go nowhere. So if you put 2 hours of work into your business for 365 days, that would be 730 hours a year, which becomes 30 days of work! Over time, your investment will pay off and all of those hours that you spent will immediately become valuable to you, far more than any time that you would spend wasting on other things.

It can be hard to look at working for free in those quiet hours as a worthy investment of time and it can be very discouraging when you aren't making any money, but let's face it, there's only one way to reach true success in the life of an artist operator and that is being willing to put in the time and energy to work on your project.

Do you treat your time as the most precious resource that you have? Or do you just let it slip away? When you are the owner of a start-up company, you must realize that time is the only resource that you are loaded with. Money is often tight when it comes to starting these new endeavors, yet we all have the exact same amount of time. If you are willing to treat your time with respect and spend as much of it as you can on your business, then it will pay off in spades. If you treat your business as a side project, or continually delay because you would rather waste your time on things that don't pay off in the long run, you might find yourself years away from your goals. The harder you work now, the more successful you will be in the future. And the best part is that once you reach a certain level of success, you will have way more free time in your life. If you invest your time properly right now, you will get double your investment back at some point, because when you work full time and are making money on your job, you don't have to worry about squirreling away each spare hour that you have.

Principle Four: Treat your art like a real job

One of the draws behind being an artist is definitely the fact that it affords you an alternative type of lifestyle. While many workers might spend most of their time doing drudgery, you are given the opportunity to enjoy every moment of what you do. Whether writing, painting or creating, there is usually a great amount of pleasure to be had in the act of creation and it can be very enjoyable. The fact that we look at these activities as escapes and pleasures can sometimes pull us away from the reality that what we are doing is actually work.

This type of interaction with our creative endeavor usually leaves us in a place of treating our work as if it were a type of recreation instead of hard work. We do it when we feel like we're in the mood, we avoid it when we're fussy or bored. Sometimes we put long hours in because we're in the zone and sometimes we might not touch it for days or even weeks at a time. This type of moodiness comes with the territory of being an artist, but if we're not careful, it can actually become an excuse that can cripple us.

If we want to become artist operators, then we must be willing to treat every aspect of what we do as a job. The biggest part of that would be to start looking at organizing your life around your job. This means that you should have a schedule that dictates where and when you work each day, so that you are able to get a lot of things done. As humans, we are ultimately creatures of habit and once you get into the rhythm of a certain kind of work, you will most likely keep that rhythm until you are interrupted.

If you wonder why it is that you aren't able to get anything done professional, the danger might lie within how you treat your schedule. Just like with a day job, you shouldn't treat it as an optional endeavor. Adhering to your schedule must be your number one priority, because if you don't adhere to the schedule, you will end up behind. A day missed becomes three days, three days becomes a week and the next thing you know, you could be out two weeks simply because you didn't want to adhere to a schedule.

There is a serious, professional benefit to adopting a schedule as well: it helps bring on the creative moods and energies. One mistake that should be avoided at all costs is believing that we should wait to be in the right kind of mood to get our work done, truthfully, moods are fickle and fleeting things. It would be foolish to put our trust in emotions to get a business taken care of.

Imagine how it would sound if a CEO were to go into work one morning and announce to his employees that he will only work when he feels like it. Not only would that create a massive uncertainty in the employees, it will also throw the company into chaos.

You are the CEO of your own company. Don't let your emotions sit in the captain's chair. There are things within a job that are very rewarding and then there are things that can be unrewarding. Don't make the mistake of only working when the job is rewarding, because that is what will prevent you from reaching the success that you so desperately desire. The reason there are very few success stories in the artist operator world is because there is a great amount of self-denial that is required if you want to get to the top. Being able to force yourself to sit down for a set amount of time each and every day is a tremendous sacrifice and there are a lot of times when it's going to suck, but by doing so, you will get ahead of the game in ways that you would never have dreamed of.

Business Principle Five: No One Is Going To Do It For You

No one is going to do it for you. These are harsh words, but the sooner you are willing to accept them, the better. The truth is, if you want to become successful as an artist operator, as an entrepreneur who is able to make a lot of money doing what you love, then you must know that no one else is going to be successful for you. This is the one big disadvantage when it comes to running the show yourself. When you are working for someone else, they are the ones who absorb all of the risk. They are the ones to give you the orders, but they are also the ones who have everything to lose when it comes to success.

By making the transfer from starving artist to artist operator, you are choosing to take your destiny in your own hands. This is no small task, however, because it is placing you in a position of power and authority. Not only does it make you the sole leader and captain of your ship, it also means that your success is entirely dependent upon you. Remember, the starving artist is the one who is striving for discovery, he is willing to put his fate into the hands of others to survive. If you aren't careful, even if you take upon the mantle of being the artist operator, you might end up subconsciously hoping for others to achieve your success for you.

    The truth is, you are the only person responsible for your success because you are the only one who cares about your product and your dream the most. No one else would ever be able to treat what you are creating or building with the same level of passion, excitement and enthusiasm. This isn't to say that you can't get help along the way or that you shouldn't partner up with other people, but rather you must be willing to accept that you have the full responsibility on your shoulders. At the end of the day, your business dream will succeed because of you or it will fail because of you. It is a heavy burden to bear, but it is true. No one is going to be successful for you. No one will make you wake up in those early hours to get your ambition done before you have to go to your day job. No one will check in to see if you are working instead of watching Netflix late at night. No one is going to ask you what your sales goals are and then hold you accountable to them. You and you alone are responsible for what you do with your dreams.

Okay, so hopefully at this juncture you should be looking at yourself as a business owner and you should have the right kind of mindset to approach how to become successful in the creative field. Now, let's turn our attention to the more practical areas: distribution and marketing.

Chapter 4: The Wonder Twins of the Digital Revolution

There are two elements that will determine your success as an artist operator. These two elements have *nothing* to do with the quality, composition, likability or enjoyability of what you create. These elements are purely business terms, but as we've learned, if we want to be successful than we must master the business portion of our work. So what then are these two elements? In two words they are Marketing and Distribution. Let's break each one down so that we can better understand them.

Distribution refers to the act of getting your product into the hands of other people. No matter what method you choose, you need some kind of distribution if you are going to get your product to the masses. There are many different types of distribution, all with various costs, benefits and consequences and we'll cover them all in detail later.

Marketing refers to the act of making people aware of your product. A lot of times we can perceive the act of marketing as some kind of sleazy, salesmanship designed to trick people into parting with their hard earned money, but that is only a type of a marketing. Truthfully, any kind of attempt to make a customer aware of your product is a kind of marketing. We'll also be covering marketing methods in a little bit.

Before we dive into these two elements deeper, you must come to recognize that these are the two most essentially pieces of running any business. Distribution lets you get your product to people and marketing makes sure that people become aware of your product so they can order it. Without either of these two, you will never be successful as a business.

So that means you must be willing to put as much time and effort as you possibly can into these two areas. Gaining mastery of these elements will guarantee that you will find some degree of success in the future. Therefore, you will want to focus on each of these areas in totality. Let us go ahead and start with distribution.

Distribution:

There are two primary types of distribution, physical and digital. In the past, physical distribution would require for you to create a bulk amount of the product, which you would then attempt to sell in order to make a profit. The problem, however, was that most of the time an artist couldn't afford all of the upfront costs and so would need a publisher to absorb the costs for them. The publisher was the one taking all of the risk and as such, they would reap most of the profits for themselves.

Digital distribution is relatively newer on the scene and it is singularly changing the way that we consume media. The eBook, the MP3 and peer-to-peer sharing systems have completely changed the name of the game. Digital distribution is instantaneous, low cost and extremely user friendly. Unlike physical distribution which would require the creation of a physical product that would have to be assembled by some costly method, digital distribution takes literally 0 dollars to create. Sure, there are things like server cost and fees associated with selling a product online, but for the most part digital distribution has replaced traditional distribution.

There is also a hybrid type of digital distribution which blends physical and digital together, this is known as On-Demand distribution. Essentially On-Demand distribution means that a product is available to be purchased online, but only when the buyer clicks the buy button, the product is then made. This means that you don't have to spend a ton of money on creating products in the hopes of selling them, rather you can create these products as they are bought.

There are different types of customers that you can choose to distribute to as well. For the sake of this book, we're going to assume that you are only engaging in business to consumer distribution, meaning that you are selling your goods directly to a consumer. There are other types of distribution, but those would fall out of the DIY style that we are developing here.

Now, then, with these different types of distribution available, we must ask, what distribution type is right for me? Thankfully, we access to all sorts of different online hubs that grant us the different types of distribution that we are looking for. Of course, nothing comes without a price and most of these hubs usually take a percentage off the top of whatever your sales are. That shouldn't discourage you, however, because the percentage that they take is usually far less than what a publisher or an agent would snag from you. So let's look at our options for each area.

Physical Distribution Options:

Amazon:

Amazon is the largest online market and is currently responsible for singlehandedly leading a digital revolution in ways of selling products online. Thanks to Amazon, you are able to distribute your physical product through them in exchange for paying a flat fee or a percentage per sale. They offer many different options, but one popular one is to set them up as the ones responsible for fulfilling your order. So if you have a product you want to sell on Amazon, you could set the product up, and then send a bulk order to Amazon for them to put in one of their fulfillment orders, allowing for them to handle all of the packaging and shipping when your products gets ordered. A lot of sellers can find this option very convenient because it lets them focus just on selling their own product without having to handle it excessively.

Etsy:

Etsy is a trailblazer in the way of helping artisans and those who like to craft find a marketplace. Etsy allows for you to set up a shop where you can sell handcrafted, one of a kind goods to buyers, and the best part is that you can set up times for how it will take for your work to ship out. Etsy gives you the option to display unique items that can only be sold once, or even to create On-Demand products that won't be created until the purchaser finalizes the sale.

One benefit of using Etsy is the trust that it creates with users. Trust is an important piece in online sales, without trust, most buyers won't give their precious financial data because they will worry that you will either rip them off or not fulfill your end of the bargain. It is a tremendous act of faith to purchase a good from another person online, so using a clearing house like Etsy or Amazon will reinforce the fact that you are trustworthy, as these companies police themselves and makes sure that the sellers stay honest.

eCommerce Website:

You are also able to put distribution in your own hands by utilizing a website to create your own eCommerce site. This would involve you getting a website put together, with hosting and a system designed to sell products to people. You, of course, would be responsible for collecting information, maintaining the website, shipping products out and handling every aspect of customer service, but it can definitely be worth it in the long run if you are able to build up a following. The biggest pro to this is that you won't have to pay excessive fees or give up a portion of your profits to other production companies, but the biggest con is that this is usually very expensive and takes a lot of time and energy to maintain.

Digital Distribution:

There are plenty of different products that you can sell digitally, with the most popular type being eBooks, educational courses, music and even films. With the power of digital distribution, you have the power to get any product that you can think of online and make it work for you in ways that you might not have ever dreamed of. Let's take a look at each type of distribution that is available to you right now.

Amazon:

Once again, we find Amazon as one of the most promising types of digital distribution that is available on the market. Amazon has worked insanely hard to corner the eBook market and has used their massive leverage as the number one bookseller in the world as a way to assist authors and writers to get their work out there. Setting up an eBook on Amazon is incredibly easy to do and it takes very little technical expertise. They have systems designed to assist you in getting started within a matter of minutes.

Of course, they are also able to assist with distributing online music as well, but you will most likely need to go through a middleman for that.

CDBaby:

If you're looking to get your music online, then CDBaby is one of the best online distributors that you can use. They charge a flat fee per album and they can assist you in getting your music or album on all of the major distributors, such as iTunes, Amazon and Spotify. They are extremely artist friendly and even have endorsements from professionals like Macklemore, who's' responsible for the hit song Thrift Shop.

YouTube:

If you are working to achieve something in the film world, or maybe you just want to create a television show, you might be tempted to write up scripts and send them in, hoping to get discovered by some big name producer. While that would be ideal for a lot of people who are aiming towards Hollywood, we know better at this point. YouTube is the perfect way for you to get your career in the film industry going, whether you are trying to become a writer, actor or director, you can spend your time and energy creating films that could potentially gain a following on YouTube. Better yet, YouTube doesn't charge you a dime for using their service, instead they could actually be paying you if you had enough views! That's right, with YouTube's ad generation system, you could monetize your free product and not charge customers a dime.

A lot of people who have aspirations to get involved in the film world are starting to come to the same conclusion as the early stage of YouTubers once did: there is a lot of money to be made online. In fact, one insanely popular YouTuber named PewdiePie made 15 million in ad revenue in 2015 alone. That number is mind boggling when you think about. There is money to be made off of this newer format and it's not going away anytime soon.

So these are some basic types of distribution that are extremely popular thanks to the power of the internet. However, these distribution types aren't the only ones that exist. There are plenty more, but we simply don't have the time to cover them all. Make sure that you do sufficient research to find the perfect distribution method for your product and focus on making your product as accessible as possible.

Chapter 5: Marketing Makes Perfect

And now we come to the last and most important piece of the whole artist operator puzzle: marketing. Marketing is the only thing that will ensure that you can be successful in your endeavors. Now, if you aren't careful, marketing can become a gigantic black hole that threatens to absorb all of your money. There are a lot of so called marketing "gurus" out there and the only thing they will help you with is separating you from your hard earned cash.

Now, we could spend an entirely separate book talking about marketing, as it is a very dense subject matter, but we are only going to be covering the essentials that you need to get started. There are four basic areas that you absolutely must take care of if you want to be able to market your products effectively. Regardless of what you are selling, these areas must be treated with the utmost seriousness. Neglecting these four areas will prevent you from making the larger sales that you will need to be successful in the future.

Marketing Basic One: Your Web Presence

It doesn't matter what you are selling, if it's an eBook, a song, a pendant keychain or even a custom made chainsaw, you are going to need to rely on your web presence in order to be able to make sales. Even if you are working locally, you still need a web presence because it allows your customers to interact with you, even if you are not directly there.

Think of your web presence as a representative who speaks on your behalf at all times. When someone connects to your products website, or to your personal website, they are able to glean all of the important information about you without ever having to chat with you. This is indispensable when we consider the fact that people are on the internet 24/7.

Of course, it's not just enough to have a website operational, you also need to make sure that your website is one that is enjoyable, easy to use, visually appealing and directly helps a customer fulfill a need.

At the core, marketing is really just about meeting the needs of a specific type of consumer. There is someone out there who wants your product, but the only problem is that they don't know it exists. Marketing is less about trying to trick people into buying your stuff and more about helping get your product in front of them and helping them see the value of your product. Now, when I say value I'm not talking about the financial gain that you have to stand from the transaction, but rather I am talking about the value that you are adding to your customer.

At the end of the day, people are naturally self-seeking creatures and are always looking for things that make their lives better. A good sales pitch never talks about how important the product is for the company, but rather it talks about how the product adds value to the customer's life. A website should focus on helping solve the problem for the consumer, regardless of what that problem might be. In the art consumption world, most people are looking for the biggest amount of value for their buck. If they see a website for yet another fantasy novel, they might roll their eyes and keep going, but if you are able to show how your fantasy novel can appeal to them directly, you'll be solving a problem.

Sometimes there are things that customers didn't even know they wanted until you mention it. By creating a visually appealing website and a very clear call to action, you can usually help a customer suddenly realize that they really want that product. This would happen more often than you think. By having a strong web and social media presence, you are able to get plenty of exposure, but exposure alone won't make you a sale, which brings us to the next point.

Marketing Basic Two: Build Your Tribe

One of the most valuable things that you can have in the marketing world is what's known as a tribe member. A tribe member is someone who likes what you make so much that not only are they willing to consume your product, but they are also willing to show your product to other people. Tribe members are passionate individuals who love what you do and are willing to tell the entire world about you. In other words, a tribe member is a fan who advocates for you on a regular basis.

Now, in the marketing world, we would consider a tribe member to be one of the most valuable things that you can have in your arsenal, but gaining them takes a lot of time, energy and patience. In order to convert a person to your tribe, you have to have some kind of connection with them. A lot of times, product superiority is an essential ingredient to getting a tribe member, but it is not the only ingredient. There are a lot of other aspects necessary to converting someone from being a mere fan to being a part of your tribe. Let's break it down.

The first step to getting a person to cross over from being a mere fan to being an ardent follower is some kind of connection with them. In other words, they need to feel that you care about them and that you can connect with them. Take a look at the marketing methods of a lot of YouTubers and podcasters. Most of them have large amounts of fans and followers who retweet or share their content by the thousands, and why is that? Because these individuals often reach out to their fans, responding to their messages, writing them personal emails back, talking to them at conventions, etc. The personal connection that an artist has with his fans can be extremely uplifting. Most of the time, a fan will rapidly move from simply being a fan to be a tribe member when they feel heard, loved and cherished, even though you are a total stranger.

They feel a connection to you through your work, but you don't necessarily know them.

There might be a temptation, to pretend to be interested in them but only be focusing on yourself throughout the process of working to get tribe members. I would caution against that because most people are able to pick up on the lack of authenticity. If you don't have a lot of time and energy to put into social media, then you might want to rethink your priorities. Making time to connect to your followers and add value to their lives will get you to the top.

However, don't make the mistake of thinking that all you need to do is post a bunch of tweets about yourself and your product in order to gain admiration and acceptance from your fans. Truthfully, you need to talk about yourself and your product as little as possible in the early stages. There is no shortage of artists who are self-obsessed and think that they are all that. The one-sidedness of social media can also contribute to these feelings of self-importance by allowing for you to post as much as you like about yourself and no one can stop you. But the problem is that when you talk about yourself, you are not adding value to your customer.

The real takeaway in marketing is that you always need to be adding value to the other party. No matter what you do, add value. When it comes to interacting with your fans and followers online, you can add value by solving their problems, sharing content that you think they would like, talking to them about what they want to talk about and participating in dialogue.

This creates a stronger relationship between you and your people and more importantly, it shows them that you care. Once they know that you care about them as a person, most fans will then listen to what you have to sell. If they like what you are selling and they like you as a person, then they will naturally cross over into the tribe member section at some point. This is an organic process, however, and you cannot rush it or else you will run the risk of looking too greedy.

Remember, a single tribe member is better than any paid advertisement because they will have organic reach that comes from a source that isn't you. Everyone expects the manager to say that the turkey club sandwich is good, but when a customer tells everyone else that the turkey sandwich is good, they'll actually believe him.

Marketing Basic Three: The Email List

As stated before, there are dozens of different types of marketing techniques that are available at your disposal and you can find all of them easily enough, but there is one marketing technique that is the most vital to your ability to survive as a business. That marketing technique is known as an email list.

An email list is nothing more than a collection of emails of people that are potentially interested in your product. We would call these people "leads." When you have a lot of leads, it makes marketing a snap because all you have to do is send out an email to everyone letting them know about your product release, give out coupons, highlight product features, etc. Wait a second, you might be thinking, are you talking about junk mail? No! Junk mail arrives to a person unsolicited and it offers little value to them. An email list depends on one crucial thing: the customer is the one to give you their email.

When a customer voluntarily gives you an email, it is a sign of trust and it also allows you to specifically target them for marketing purposes in the future. Email lists are amazing marketing tools and they are the most important thing in your arsenal as a marketer. The reason why email lists are so useful is that they never go away. When you have a lead, until you annoy them enough to unsubscribe, you have the ability to communicate with them through email at any time you like. This allows you to directly market any product that you have. So if you collect 1,000 emails over the course of your work, whenever you have a new product release, you can send emails to all of them telling them about your product. Since they are directly part of your demographic and already trust you, you will have a higher rate of return than if you were to tweet or update people on Facebook about your product.

So if email lists are so valuable, how can you get people to sign up for one? Well, its simple enough, really. You need to have what's known as a lead generation system. Here's how the lead generation system works. First you need what's known as a lead magnet. A lead magnet is a valuable item that you are going to be giving away for absolutely free in exchange for the email address. For example, if you were a writer, you could have an eBook that is composed of a few short stories that you have written. Someone signs up for that eBook so that they can enjoy your work and then you obtain their email address to use whenever you like.

Don't underestimate the power of giving something away for free. The more perceived value that your lead magnet has for people who are looking at your website, the more emails that you will collect over time. Now, make sure that your product is valuable, no one wants to be disappointed when they get a free eBook only to discover a five page waste of time. This is the first step in building a real business relationship with your customers, so don't screw it up and don't be stingy!

If you're wondering where people will find your email list offer, the answer is that it should be on your website. The website allows for you to gather emails as people visit. If you want to get people to really focus on your offer, you might want to consider building a lead page. A lead page is a special part of your website that will allow for you to directly offer your free eBook to people and highlight all of the value that it can add to their life. This takes the distraction of the regular website away from them and leaves them only focusing on the thing right in front of them your enticing free offer which you hope will result in them to subscribing to your email list.

You will need to use a specific type of website that helps build and maintain email records, we would recommend Mailchimp as it is the easiest to use and it is very straightforward. The best part is that it's free until you reach 2,000 emails, which is no small number for someone who's just starting out. MailChimp is easy to use and intuitive, so you should definitely utilize it.

Remember, the email list is not just a part of marketing, but rather it is one of the backbones of the marketing revolution. You should be focusing a lot of energy on how to build, maintain and draw in new leads with the help of your email list. A lot of businesses get all mixed up and start focusing on building up numbers such as Facebook likes, Twitter followers, etc., but those things don't have the same power that the email list does. Your sole goal should be to build up that marketing list as much as you can, because it will deliver far better results than Facebook or Twitter could. This doesn't mean that you shouldn't grow your Facebook following or your Twitter presence, but let those be done for the purpose of boosting your email list, not for their own sake. Everything that you do online should ultimately lead people to your email list, because that is how you make sales.

Marketing Basic Four: Facebook Ads

And last, but certainly not least, we're going to talk about paid advertisements. It used to be that back in the day it was extremely expensive to have advertisements run for your products and most people would only see them through television or radio ads. But fortunately, the times have changed and in your favor! Thanks to Facebook, people spend an average of 50 minutes per day on Facebook and those 50 minutes are filled with directly tailored ads that are custom made to reach a specific type of audience.

Thanks to the power of Facebook ads, you have the ability to reach an ideal market with just the click of a button. Creating an ad is easy to do with the help of the Power Editor made by Facebook and they will let you set up what is known as Pay-Per-Click advertising. What PPC advertising means is that whenever someone sees your ad, it doesn't charge you until they actually click on the ad. You set up an initial budget and set the ad to run over a set number of days and then watch as Facebook reaches people and sells to them for you!

Do Facebook ads work? The short answer is yes! The reason they work so well is because Facebook has complex algorithms that allow for you to reach people who are part of your targeted demographic. Facebook can track behaviors, interests, likes and other things that will give you clues as to what kind of content this person consumes. For example, if someone loves Fantasy novels and you are trying to market a fantasy novel, Facebook will help you put an ad right in front of them. This will let you sell your book to the right kind of person for a nominal fee.

Facebook ads really work, but they take time and effort to develop. It is not a hard science and it is certainly not a guaranteed success formula, but with a willingness to experiment and a lot of effort and energy, you will be able to make money through selling on Facebook. Don't be fooled into thinking that it isn't worth the cost, the truth is, most good marketing will cost you money and thanks to Facebook's competitive bidding, you won't find more effective advertising anywhere else for cheaper. It doesn't take a lot to make sales or get email list conversions, just a willingness to give it a shot and be open to editing as you learn more about the system.

Conclusion

At the end of the day, being an artist operator takes a lot of hard work, effort and energy. It is not a small accomplishment to make yourself something in the world as an artist. There are millions of imitators and people who are hoping to make it in this world, but if you want to truly be the one who stands out then you have to start taking what you do seriously. Do not simply treat it as an art or a hobby, but rather treat it as the serious business that you know that it can become. And you will find that as the days, weeks and months go by, with each sale that you make, with every email acquired and with each tribe member that you gain, your business will grow in leaps and bounds. You can then say goodbye to the Starving Artist persona that has sabotaged the success and happiness of so many other artists who had skill and potential.

All it takes is for you to realize that the hard work begins after you make the product. It's a tough pill to swallow and it can be disheartening, but think about it like this. You spent a lot of time and effort on making this product and now it sits in the world, untouched by people who would *love* to consume it. You fought this hard to bring your product into the world, are you going to fight that hard to make sure that other people will be able to enjoy it too?

Other books available by Landon T. Smith on Kindle, paperback and audio:

Why NLP Isn't Working For You

The Art of Influence

The Power of Reflection: Embrace Your Past to Find a Purpose for Your Future

Meet Maslow: How Understanding the Priorities of Those Around Us Can Lead to Harmony and Improvement

Manderstanding: Learn How to Read the Cues and Understand the Motives of the Male Gender

Deconstruction Of Self: Untangling Negative Thoughts About Yourself To Rebuild A Self Of Steel

The End of Chaos: Break Away From Bad Habits, Addictions and Self Destructive Tendencies Before They Break You

Be a Boss: A Guide To Earning The Trust, Respect and Loyalty Of Those Around You

www.ingramcontent.com/pod-product-compliance
Lightning Source LLC
Chambersburg PA
CBHW020449220526
45464CB00002B/920